Rufus
and the
Rain

Written by Sarah Green

Illustrated by Frances Isaacs

AB

First published in Great Britain in 2023

Editing, design & publishing by Andrew Buller - www.andrewbuller.co.uk

Text copyright © 2023 Sarah Green - Illustration copyright © 2023 Frances Isaacs

Small illustration elements for paw prints, bones, snowflakes, feathers etc from Canva.com

All rights reserved. No part of this publication may be reproduced, stored in a retrieval system, or transmitted, in any form or by any means, electronic, mechanical, photocopying, recording or otherwise, without the prior permission of the copyright owner.

DEDICATIONS

Sarah:
"To my four boys - David, Tim, Leo,
and of course, Rufus"

Frances:
"To my husband, Barrow,
and our sons Benjamin and Edward"

ACKNOWLEDGEMENTS

Sarah: There are so many people who have helped me in my life, too numerous to mention. I thank them all. I am though particularly grateful for my stepson Tim, who is always there for me, John Sandbach, seer, poet and rock, Donny Ridge, doyenne of magical middle of the night calls which could last until dawn, Todi and Laurel Hughes, my second family, Hilary and Nick Adamson, whose door was always open, and many thanks to Liz Jennings for connecting me with Frances who so 'got' Rufus and our ever- patient publisher, Andrew.

Frances: Many thanks to Innovations in Dementia, the organisation that saved me, and in particular Rachel Niblock and Steve Milton.

FOREWORD

When Sarah wrote this wonderful children's story about Rufus and his fear of the rain, and how he faced up to his challenges, it reminded me again of how easy it is for any of us, no matter how old, to be stopped in our tracks by old fears which can seem like insurmountable obstacles.

The Tibetan word for obstacle, parche, means "what cuts our progress". Rufus found through his travels that he could cut through his rain obstacle and that it was not quite as scary and all powerful after all. And that he could have fun.

Sarah and Frances are both living with dementia, and this makes the creation of Rufus's journey even more poignant, heart-warming and inspiring.

David Green

All proceeds will be donated to support the work of Innovations in Dementia and the Jampa Ling Tibetan Buddhist Meditation Centre.

BEING OUT IN THE RAIN

"Being out in the rain is no fun
Trying to pee in the rain is the worst
I am soggy and wet
The saddest hound you have met
I think I am ready to burst."

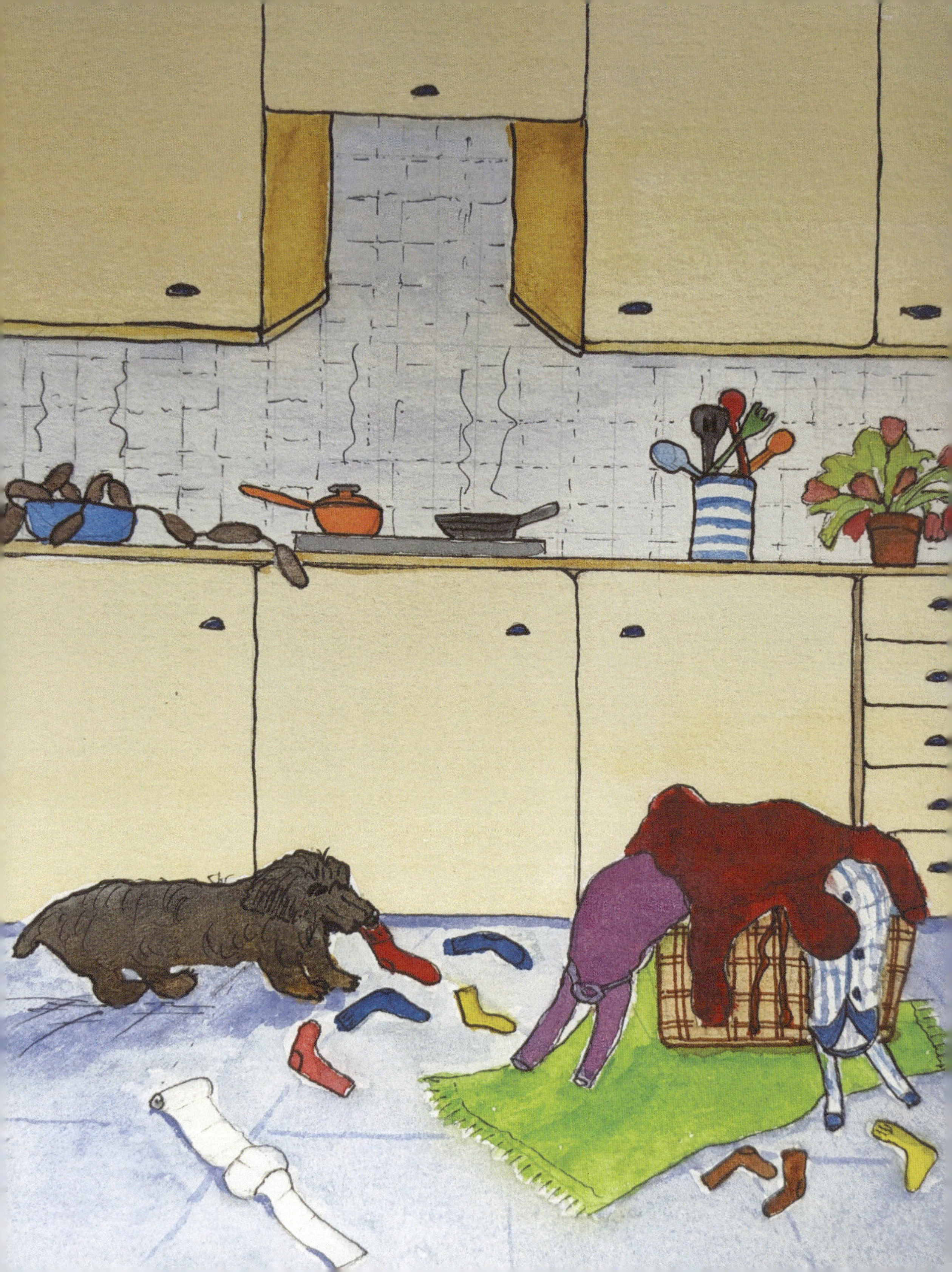

HOW IT STARTED

Rufus was having a very good day.

All his humans were out. He was having enormous fun unravelling a whole roll of toilet paper, followed by a good long chew on some very smelly socks he had found at the bottom of the laundry basket.

"Time to go and play in the garden," he thought.

He looked out of the window. What a drag. It was raining. That was not good. Rufus, a very small and scruffy, wire-haired dachshund, totally hated being out in the rain. He could see his new neighbour, Christopher, a tall and hairy Irish wolfhound, having a great time outside. Christopher adored the rain. He loved charging around, jumping in puddles, chewing on soggy sticks and woofing at the top of his lungs. Getting wet did not bother him at all.

"Why on earth would a dog want to play in the rain?" thought Rufus. He didn't know why he hated the rain. He just did. He always had. It made him feel totally miserable and he would tremble from head to tail.

So, Rufus went back to chewing the smelly socks.

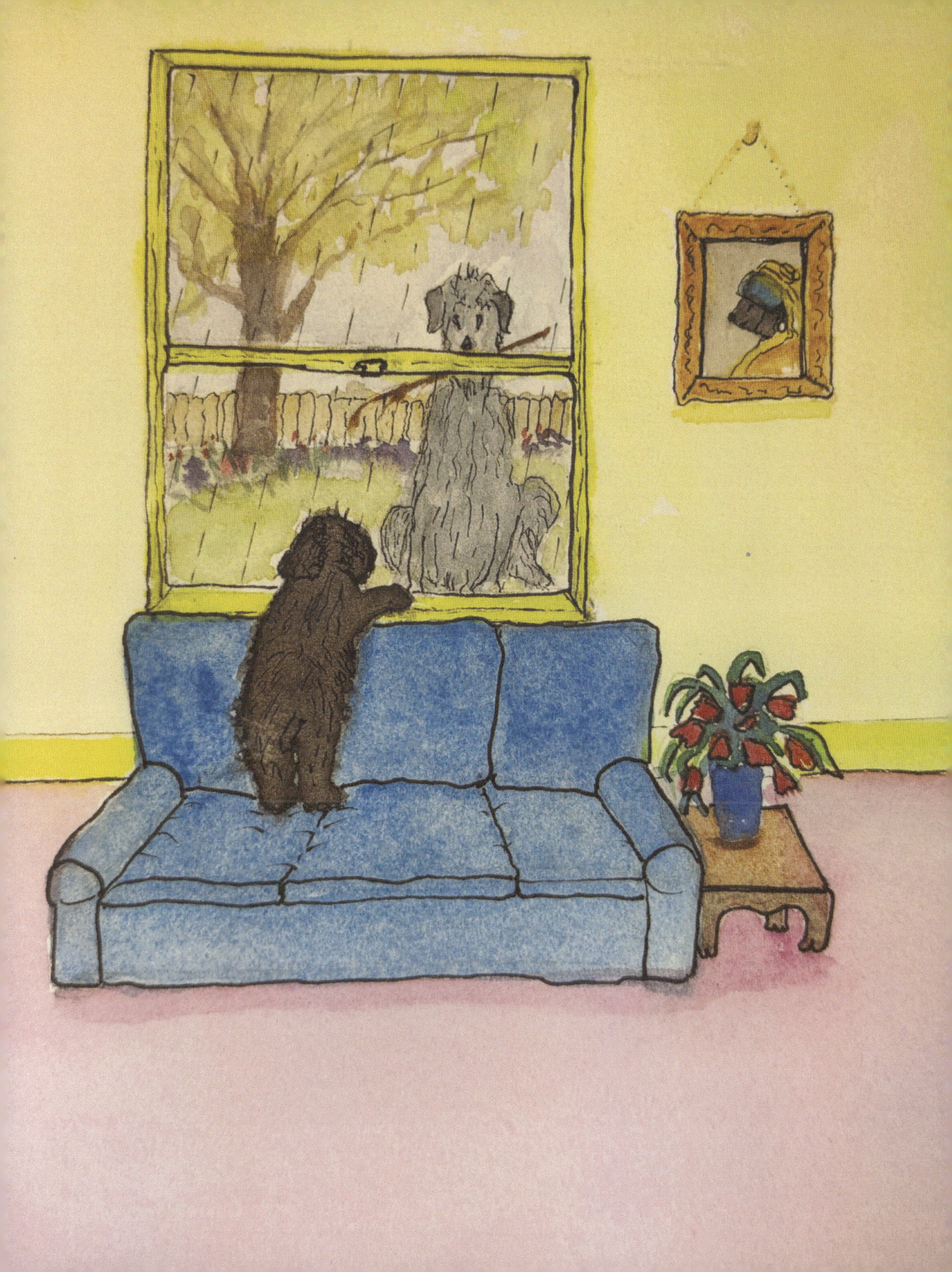

The next afternoon the rain had stopped and the two dogs were playing outside. "Why didn't you come out and play yesterday, you missed all the fun?" asked Christopher.

"Well, I'm rather afraid of the rain," replied Rufus. "In fact, I hate the rain. I really, really, really don't like getting wet. Not one bit."

"Hmm, maybe you should talk to Bones..."

"Bones? Who's Bones? Is Bones a dog?"

"Sure he is. Bones helps lots of dogs with all sorts of problems. He can help you with anything. Just get your iPaw and hit the red button. A voice will ask 'How can I help you?' That will be Bones. Tell him your problem and he'll sort you out for sure."

When he got home Rufus decided to have a go. He so wanted to play in the rain with Christopher. He found his iPaw in his basket and hit the red button.

Sure enough... "Hi Rufus," said a voice. "This is Bones. How can I help you?"

"So, Bones," said Rufus nervously, "I hate the rain and I am afraid to play outside with my friend Christopher when it is raining. He has so much fun and I want to have fun too. Can you help me?"

"Sure," replied Bones. "Just relax. Help will be with you very soon. And don't worry Rufus -

in no time at all you will be having fun with Christopher, whatever the weather."

"Thank you Bones," said Rufus. "I am so excited."

"Wow, that sounds very easy," thought Rufus. "I do hope it rains tomorrow."

So, Rufus curled up on the old blue sofa in the kitchen, his iPaw beside him, and waited for help to arrive.

None came. He waited some more. He started to think about eating, eating his favourite food - sausages. "Four pork sausages would be the best meal in the world," he thought. He stretched out on the sofa, feeling very happy, and rather sleepy...

EAMONN THE EAGLE

"Hi Rufus. My name is Eamonn. I am your help," boomed a very deep voice.

Rufus nearly jumped out of his fur.

Standing in front of him was a huge bird. Really huge. Black, with a ginormous, yellow beak and piercing yellow eyes. A bright, white head. And his feet were red.

This bird was seriously scary.

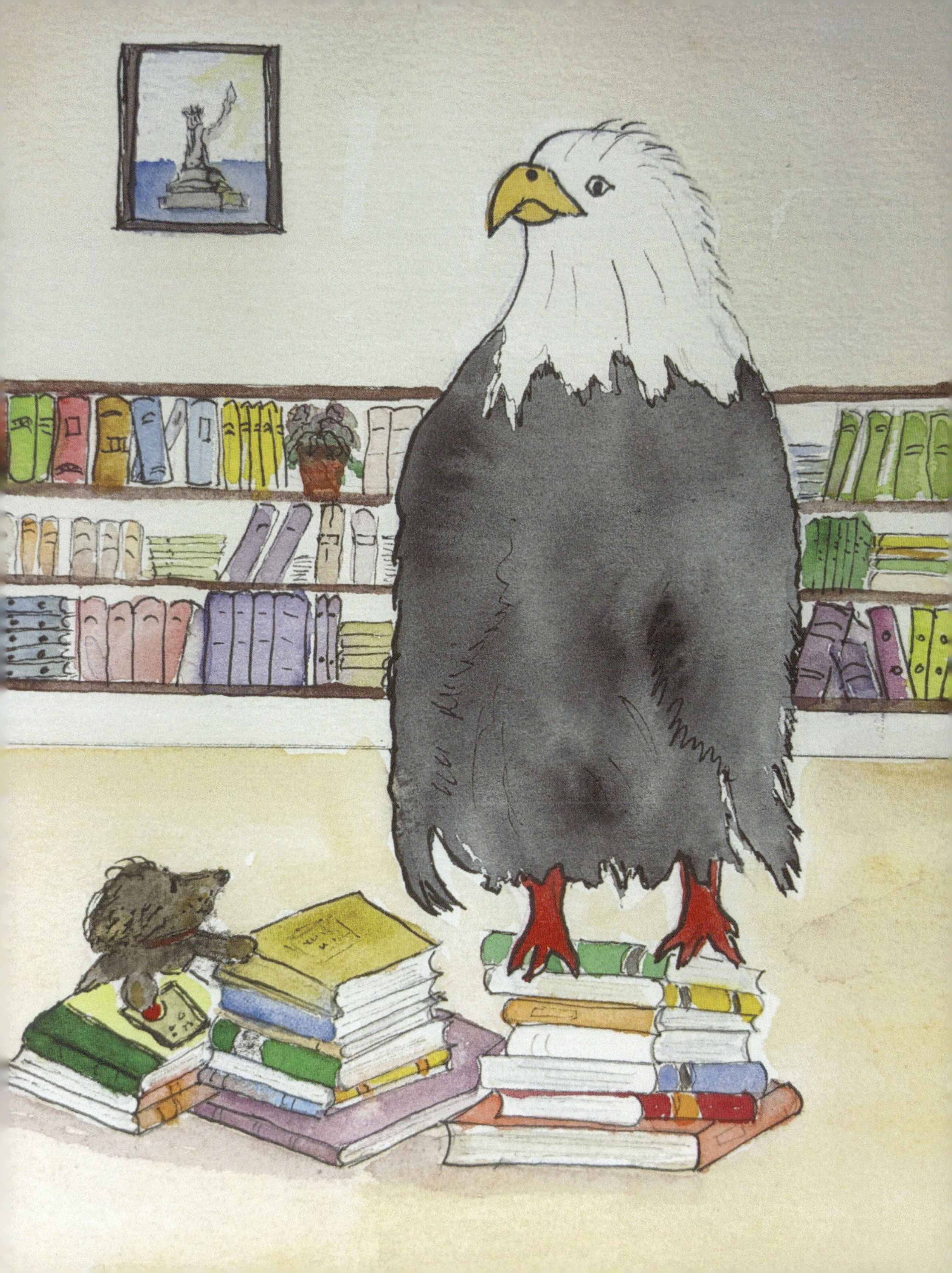

Rufus didn't feel good. He hoped that Eamonn could not hear the gurgling noises coming from his tummy.

"I think there must be a mistake. I mean you don't look like help. I need to talk to Bones." And Rufus ran behind the sofa, trembling from head to tail. He tapped the red button on his iPaw.

"Please tell me Bones that this super scary bird called Eamonn is not my help?"

"Eamonn is my best helper," replied Bones. "If he is the first eagle you have ever met, he may seem scary. But he is really very kind and very gentle. If you ask, he might even roll on to his back and let you scratch his tummy! And he is very ticklish!"

"Not in a million years!" thought Rufus.

"So, Rufus," Bones continued, "I am sending you on a series of adventures with Eamonn as your guide. Eamonn is a great adventurer, always ready for new experiences, new places, new people. See how you feel about the rain when you get home."

This didn't sound good to the little dachshund. "I don't want new anything," he thought. "I just want everything to stay the way it is... without the rain of course. And I do wish I could stop trembling!"

"Couldn't you wave a magic wand or something Bones - or maybe say some magic words and make my fear of the rain disappear?"

"But you'd miss all the fun you are going to have," was the reply. "And, if at any time, you want to stop an adventure, press the home button on your iPaw and you will be back home in the blink of an eye. Or just say sausages if you want to feel better. Anyway, time you were off!"

"OK, hop on my back Rufus, and put your paws round my neck. Hang on, and off we go," said Eamonn. Rufus nervously scrambled up Eamonn's left wing and wrapped his paws around the eagle's neck. And, before he could say sausages, Eamonn spread his wings and soared high into the sky.

"Ooooooo," whimpered Rufus, his eyes tight shut.

"OK back there young dog - what do you see?" asked Eamonn.

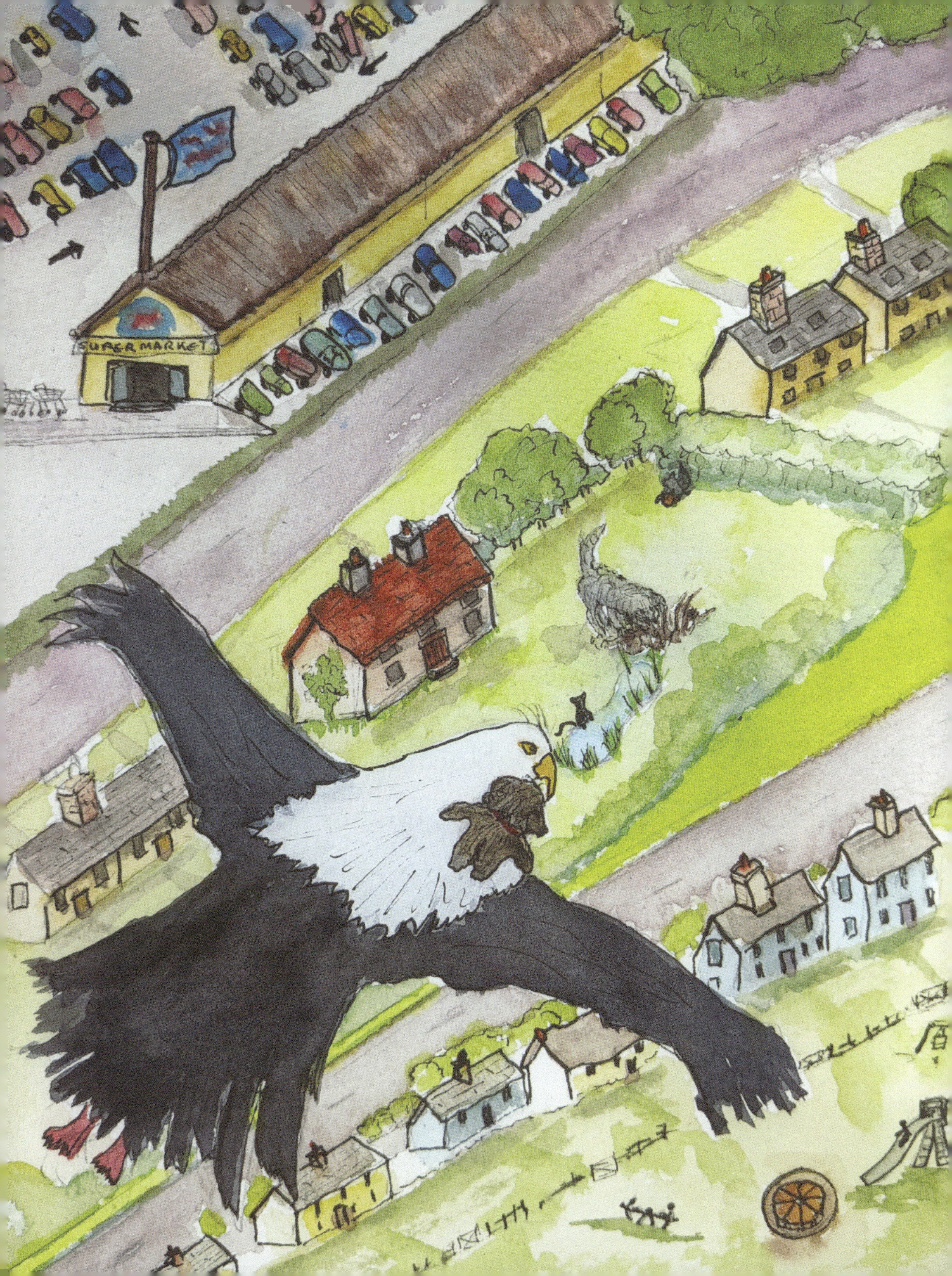
SUPERMARKET

"I can't see anything," said Rufus, "because my eyes are shut tight. I am so scared. I don't like this adventure. I want to go home."

"You can hold onto me as tightly as you like, but I want you to open your eyes, look down and tell me what you see."

Rufus slowly opened one eye. Then the other. And looked down. He blinked, and blinked again.

"Oh my goodness, I know exactly where we are," he said, as they flew over a red tin roof. "That's my home." He could see BeBe the cat sitting by the fish pond cleaning her whiskers and keeping an eye on the fish, Christopher enthusiastically digging a hole, and Nutjob the squirrel running across the lawn with the biggest acorn ever.

"Wow, this is super cool," he thought. "I am home. Yippee, the adventure must be over!"

"Thank you Eamonn. This has been a great adventure seeing my home and my friends from high in the sky. Perhaps you could put me down now?"

"Put you down?! Rufus, our adventures have only just begun. So get ready to fly higher, and further, and faster."

And they did fly higher and further and faster. Over mountains and valleys, forests and plains, lakes and rivers and oceans.

They waved to lots of people, to birds and animals galore...

"So, what do you think of this amazing world you live in Rufus?"

"It's magic," was the response. And it was magic - he wasn't frightened anymore. He was excited. He was having fun. And his stomach had stopped gurgling, thank goodness!

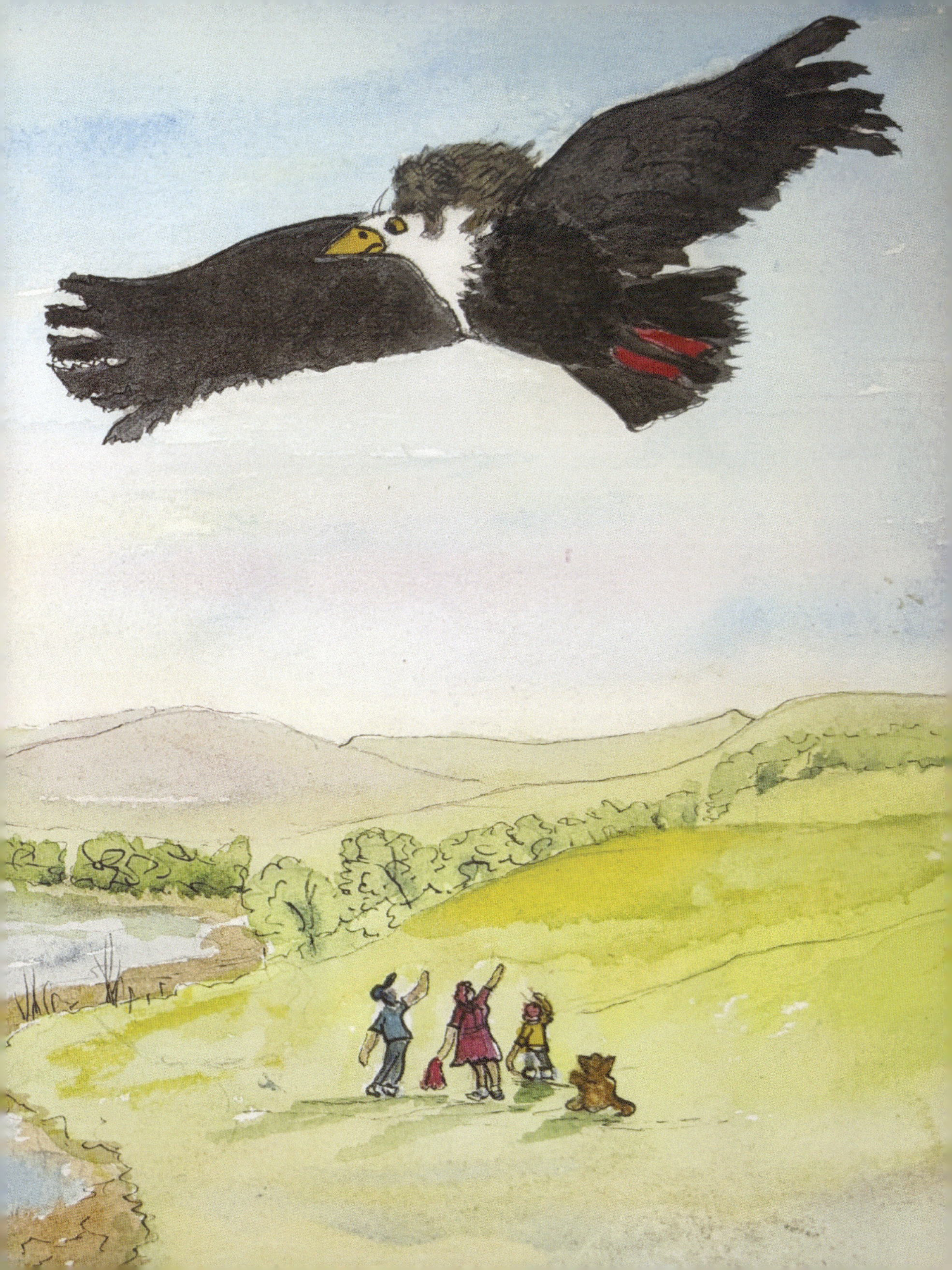

THE WHITE WORLD

Rufus suddenly noticed that he was feeling cold - actually very cold. "Eamonn, I can't stop sh-shivering and sh-shaking."

"Well, that's because we have come to the Arctic, and it is cold in the Arctic. In a short while you won't even notice. We've come here so you can meet a very good friend, Petronella. She is a very smart polar bear," explained Eamonn.

All Rufus could see below him was white. It looked like snow. And ice. "That's not so bad," thought Rufus, "cos I like the snow." He noticed, as he climbed down from Eamonn's back that, even though it was very cold, the cold wasn't bothering him anymore.

"So, where do we meet Petronella?" he asked, feeling a bit better.

"Here she comes now," said Eamonn.

"Where?" asked Rufus.

"There," said Eamonn.

"There is where?" said Rufus.

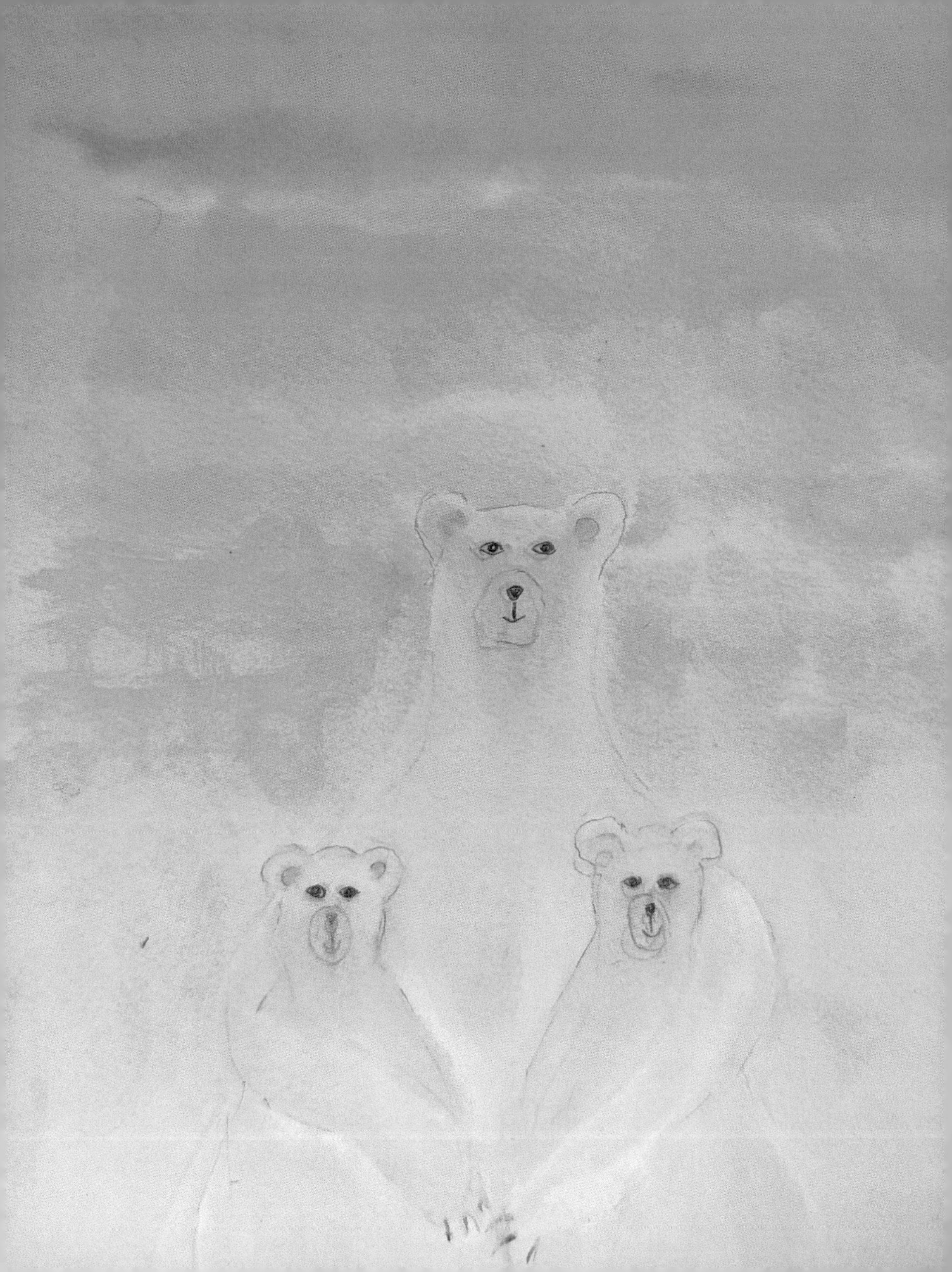

And sure enough, right in front of him, out of the white, he could see some black spots. Moving closer. Growing larger. And they weren't spots. He saw that they were black eyes and black noses! Belonging to three white furry animals. One was very big, bigger than his humans at home, and two were smaller. Coming closer and closer.

Keep calm Rufus, think of sausages, he said to himself as he hid behind Eamonn.

"Hi Rufus, I think I see you hiding behind Eamonn," said the largest of the white, furry animals. "I'm Eamonn's friend, Petronella and I am a polar bear. These are my twin cubs Leo and Lily. A big welcome to our home."

"We're so excited you are here", said Leo. "Do come swimming with us. We have been so looking forward to playing in the water with you. It will be such great fun."

"Good grief, they swim here - in that icy water," thought Rufus. "They must be bonkers."

Suddenly things didn't feel much fun any more. "Sausages, sausages, sausages," he whispered. It didn't help.

"Come and join us as quickly as you can," said Lily, as the cubs scampered off.

By now Rufus was shaking and his legs felt like jelly. In fact, he was scared that his legs would give out, and he'd fall flat on his face!

"It's no good Eamonn - I need to go home. It's time to push the home button on my iPaw. This is just too scary. Icy water. Big white bears. And all that talk of swimming - just too much!"

"The cubs would love you to join them Rufus," said Petronella, "but don't feel you have to swim today."

"Oh thank you so much," said Rufus with a sigh of relief. "You see, I don't like getting wet in the rain, or being in water, and I can't swim. So, I don't think I'll have a go today. This has already been a big adventure for me, and I am rather tired."

"Very smart of you," Petronella replied. "You'll know when you are ready to learn to swim. Just watch Leo and Lily today. It will be fun."

And it was fun watching the cubs playing - diving under water, racing, swimming forwards and backwards, performing all sorts of tricks. Rufus had to admit that he would love to be happy in the water like Lily and Leo. He so wished he could swim like them.

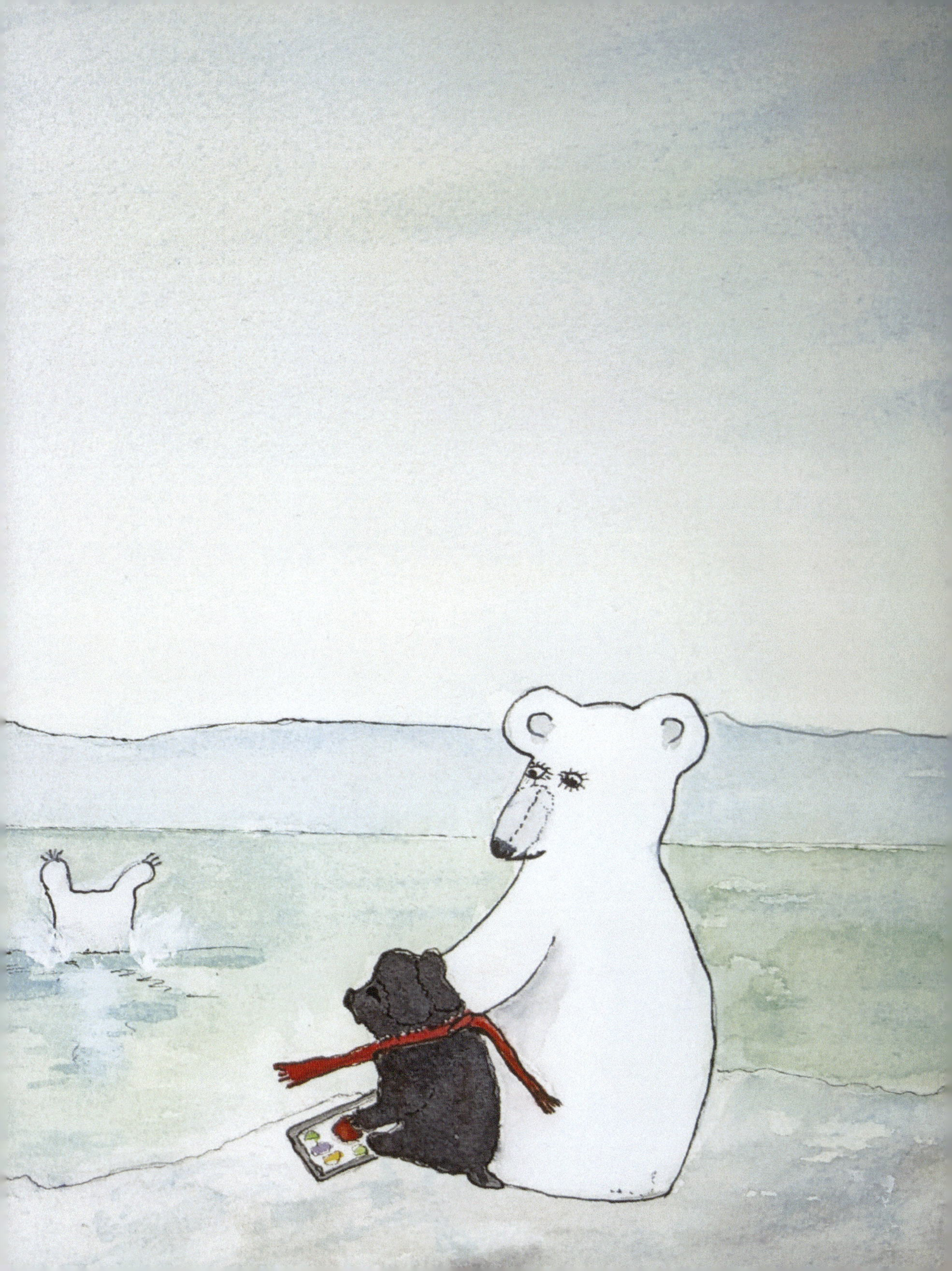

Eventually, it was time to leave, and they said their goodbyes. Rufus climbed onto Eamonn's back, still clutching his iPaw, and away they flew.

As Rufus looked back, the polar bears were lying on their backs, basking in the afternoon sun. Rufus was sad to leave.

"I do like snow, but what exactly is it Eamonn?"

"Frozen water," came the reply.

"Oh," thought Rufus.

AND THEN IT WAS GREEN

"Ready for the next adventure?" asked Eamonn.

"Another adventure? I hope this one is not too scary. What if I don't get back home in time for breakfast?" thought Rufus, "What will my humans think? If I go on another adventure I might be away so long that they totally forget about me. But, on the other hand, another adventure might be OK... as long as I get home before everyone wakes up... and in time for breakfast..."

"I am ready Eamonn, as long as it is somewhere warm, and I get home before my family wake."

"You'll be home in plenty of time Rufus, and you are most certainly going to be warm."

And it was not long before all Rufus could see was a sea of green - green tree tops. And he was definitely feeling a good deal warmer!

"Where are we Eamonn?"

"High up in the forest. This will be a fun adventure. You are going to meet another good friend. So hold on tight Rufus, we are about to land." And land they did on a very high branch of a very tall tree - so tall, with such thick branches that Rufus could not see the ground.

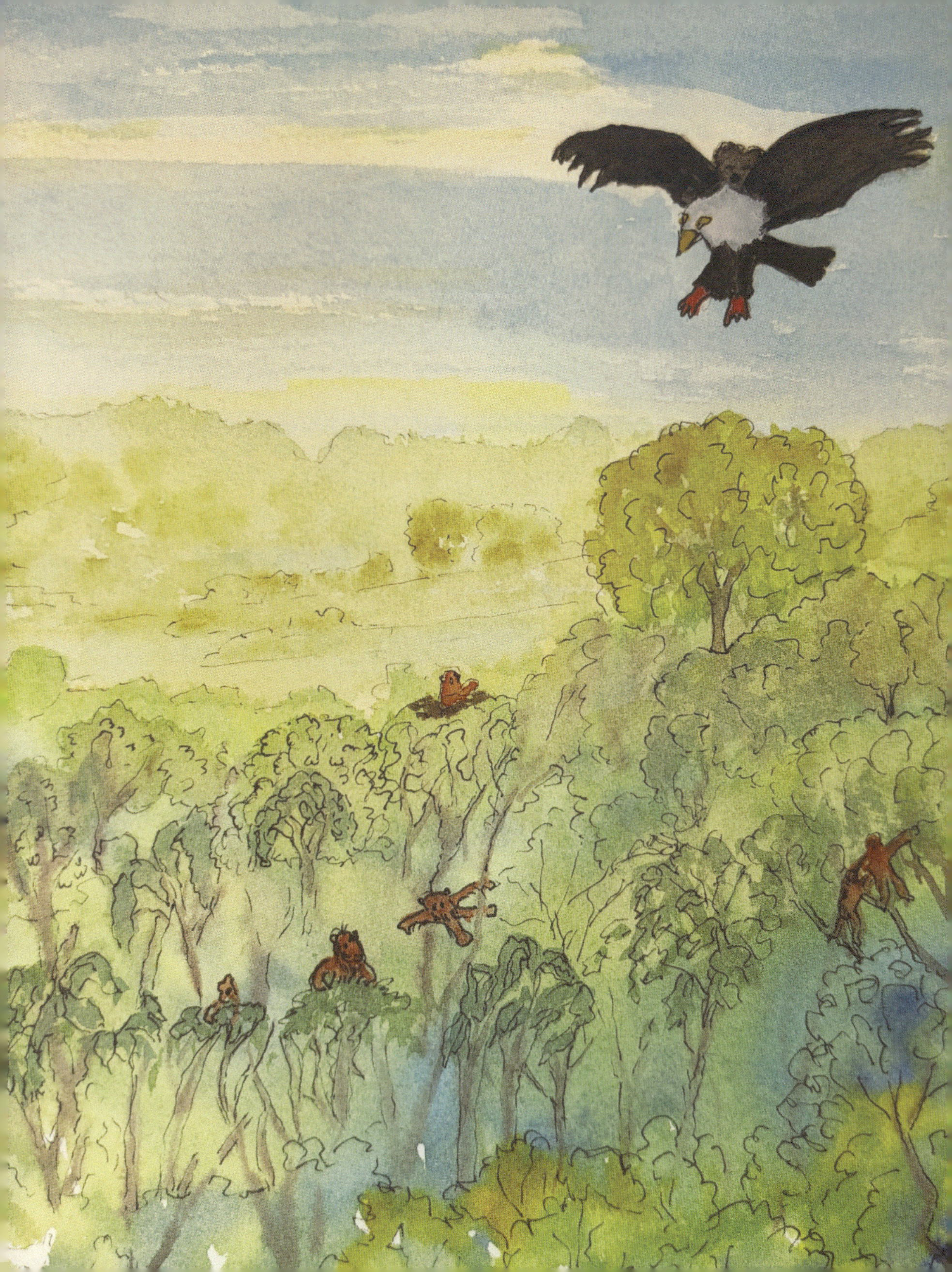

"Sit tight Rufus," said Eamonn, "we are waiting for PappaO."

"PappaO - what sort of name is that?"

"It's a very fine name," boomed a deep voice from somewhere beneath them. And up popped a head. An extraordinary head with long red hair. The head turned and Rufus guessed that he was looking into the face of PappaO - a face with the gentlest of eyes and warmest of smiles. And the next minute PappaO was sitting on a branch beside them.

"Rufus, welcome to the rain forest, home of orangutans," said PappaO. "We are meeting in the tree tops because we are tree dwellers. We rarely need to go down to the ground at all."

"Rain forest! Not going down to the ground!"

Rufus felt faint. His head was spinning. His heart was pounding.

This was definitely the time to hit that home button...

"Very good to meet you PappaO," replied Rufus. "I do love your red hair. Umm, I was thinking that maybe we could spend our time together on the ground. I am worried that I might fall and never be seen again."

"I won't let you fall, I promise," said PappaO.

"But this is the rain forest - and I bet it must rain a lot if it's called that. You see, I am super frightened of the rain."

"No worries my little friend," came the gentle reply, "when it does rain, I will show you how to stay totally dry. Look, Eamonn is off to see some friends and while he is away we are going to do some tree travel. So, relax my young friend, and enjoy the ride."

Before he could think of anything else to say, Rufus found himself on the back of the orangutan, holding on tightly. They started to swing through the forest, from branch to branch, vine to vine. Slipping slowly and easily through this green world, Rufus began to relax.

"That's good," said PappaO, "just hang loose - it's hot in the rain forest."

After a while the orangutan stopped for a rest, and asked if Rufus wanted something to eat or drink. "I'm not thirsty, but I am hungry. Do you have any dog biscuits?"

"No, but I can offer you some tree bark," replied PappaO, stripping a piece off a tree trunk and handing it to the little dog. It tasted delicious.

"OK Rufus, it is going to rain and we need to take shelter." PappaO reached for two enormous leaves, one of which he gave to the dachshund. "Shelter under this, it will keep you totally dry."

And sure enough, even though the rain was heavy, they did stay dry.

"How can you live in a place with so much rain?" asked Rufus.

"Easy, I love it. I love watching the rain and I love how it sounds. And, if I want to take a shower or I want to cool down, I just let myself get wet. And, if I am thirsty, I can use a leaf to collect water. It's easy."

"Wow, that does sound easy," thought Rufus, "I can see that if I lived here I just might get used to the rain, and to getting wet!"

"Do you want to try a rain forest shower?"

"Not today, thank you PappaO, but it has stopped raining. Can we do some more tree travel?"

"I wish we could, but I can hear Eamonn calling. Sadly it must be time for you to leave. Our time together has gone far too fast." He was right. The time had zoomed by.

Rufus climbed on to PappaO's back. They swung up through the trees to where Eamonn was waiting. It had been a magical time and Rufus hadn't thought about sausages once!

"Come back and see us Rufus," said PappaO.

"I will for sure," said the little dachshund, as he gazed into the eyes of this wonderful animal for the last time. "I have so loved my time in the rain forest." The next minute the gentle orangutan had disappeared underneath the tree tops. Rufus was sad to see him go.

THE SWIMMING PARTY

"One last stop, and then home Rufus. So, climb aboard." And they were away.

In no time at all they were standing by a large lake, with more water than Rufus had ever seen in his life. "We are here to meet some Asian elephants," said Eamonn, "and look, here they are." Coming towards them were the largest creatures Rufus had ever seen. Legs as thick as tree trunks. Twice as tall as any human. And their noses - well their noses were the longest you could imagine.

"Hello Rufus," said one of the huge creatures, "my name is Betsy and I would like you to meet my family. This is my son Jojo," pointing her long nose at a very small elephant standing beside her. Everyone else seemed to be either a sister, an aunt, a nephew, or a niece. And there were cousins galore.

"We were so excited to hear from Bones that you were coming to visit us. So, we decided to have a swimming party. Eamonn, are you joining us?"

"I am going to have a siesta Betsy if you don't mind. We have been doing a lot of flying."

"Hurrah," said Jojo, running over to Rufus. "Swimming is my favourite thing. We are going to have so much fun."

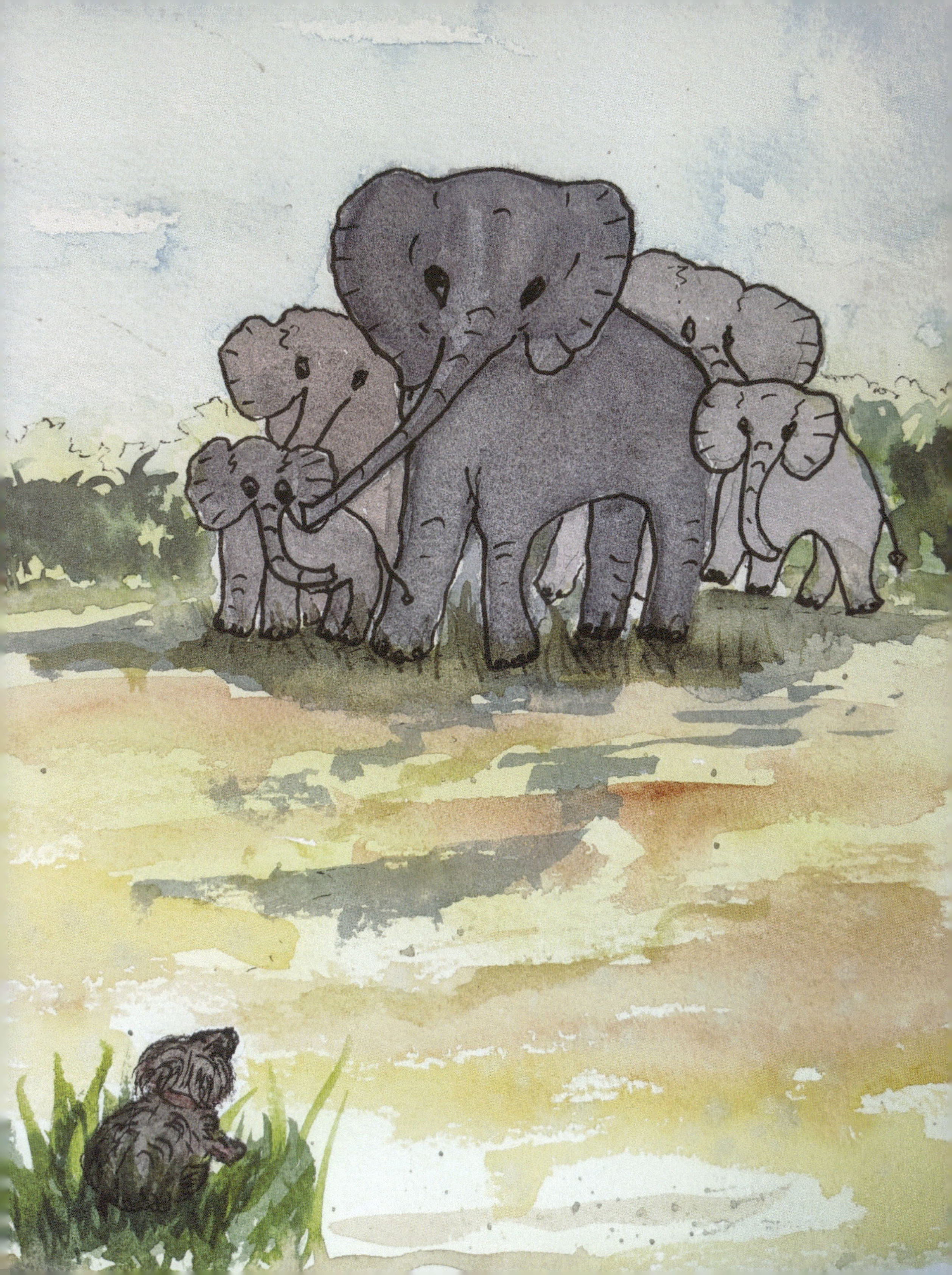

"Well, I have never actually swum before," said Rufus, in a very small voice. "Maybe Jojo, if you or any of your cousins are going to have a swimming lesson I could watch and have a go another time."

"But Rufus, we all swim. Everyone knows how to swim."

"Oh dear," thought Rufus. "Maybe I should have got in the water with Leo and Lily. I am going to feel rather silly."

"Well, if you don't mind Jojo, I will sit here on the bank and watch you all."

At that moment Betsy came up. "I have an idea," she said to Rufus.

Before he knew what was happening, Betsy had lifted him up with her extraordinary nose and he was sitting on her back, able to see all around him. Rufus felt very important, as he watched all the elephants coming down to the water, and starting to party.

"Betsy," said Rufus, "I hope it is not a rude question, but why do you have such a long nose?"

"Good question," laughed Betsy. "Our noses are called trunks, as they look not unlike the trunk of a tree. We use them for lots of things. We use them to suck up water like this," said Betsy, spraying the water in the air. "And to grab food. I could tell you so much more about our fabulous trunks, but how do you feel about the swimming party?"

"Everyone seems to be having a great time," said Rufus, as he watched all the elephants playing in the water.

He wished he could join in. It looked fun as they used their trunks to splash each other. Lots and lots of fun.

"Let's try something," said Betsy. She reached up with her trunk, picked up the little dog, and gently lowered him to the ground. They walked to the water's edge.

"Do you feel like testing the water Rufus?"

Rufus dipped his front paws in the water. It felt good. Nice and warm, not cold like in the Arctic.

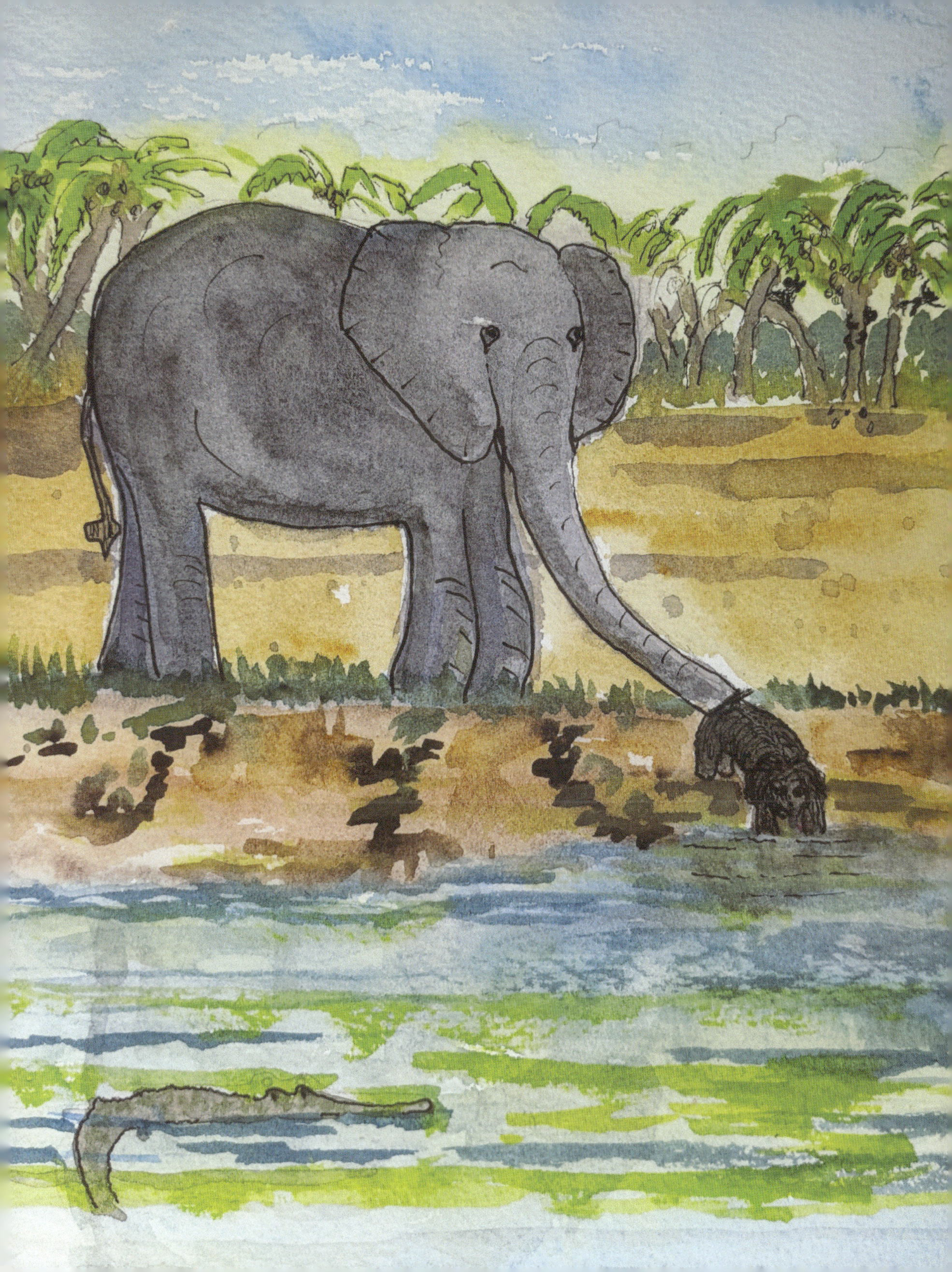

"Do you think you could go deeper?" asked Betsy. "Here, sit on my trunk," which she had curled into a seat.

Rufus climbed aboard, and Betsy slowly walked into slightly deeper water. Even more slowly, she lowered Rufus into the water, as he sat on her trunk.

"How's that?" she asked.

"It feels good," said a small voice.

They went a little deeper, and then a little deeper still.

"How would you like to have a go on your own?" asked Betsy after a while, "and then you could play with Jojo and his cousins."

Rufus looked across, and could see the little elephants having a great time playing with a large red ball. He thought about the fun he had had watching Leo and Lily playing in the icy water. Hanging loose in the rain forest with PappaO had been very cool. And flying with Eamonn had opened up a whole new world. So, swimming didn't seem like such a big deal anymore.

"Maybe I could have a go on my own," said Rufus.

So, Betsy walked back to shallower water. She slowly removed her trunk. Suddenly, Rufus was paddling in the water. Somehow he knew how to swim. Betsy's trunk was gone and it was all OK.

Rufus was swimming. And smiling. And happy.

And the rest of the afternoon was spent playing water games with Jojo and his cousins.

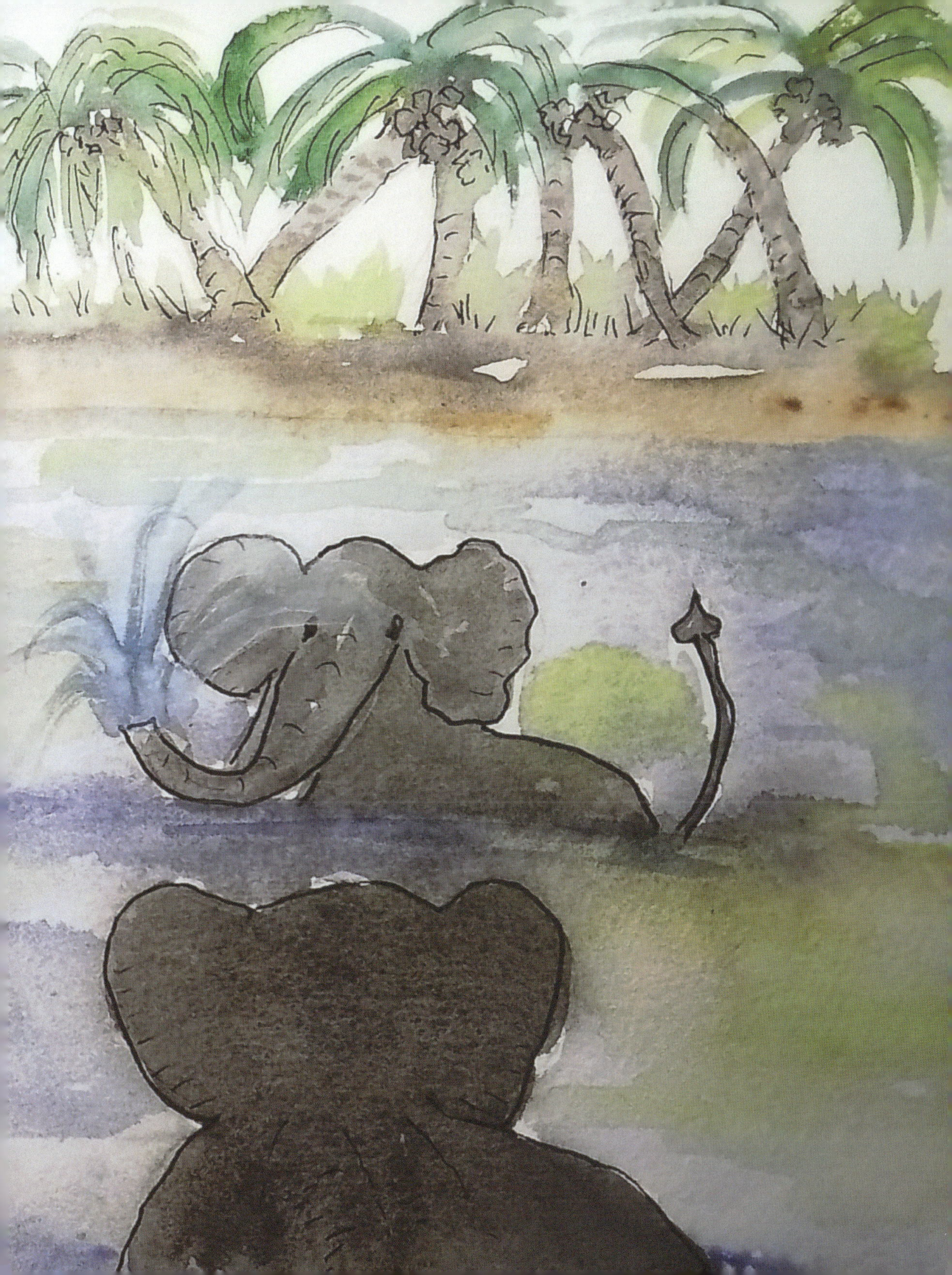

All too soon the party was over and it was time to leave. Rufus said goodbye to the elephants and thanked Betsy and Jojo for the party.

"I really don't want to leave Eamonn," said Rufus sadly, as he climbed onto the eagle's back. "Can't we stay longer?"

"You really are an excellent adventurer Rufus, and I have so enjoyed our time together. However, it is time to go home. Remember, you need to be back in your kitchen before the family wake up. So hit that home button on your iPaw and let's go..."

HOME AGAIN

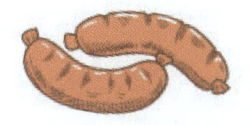

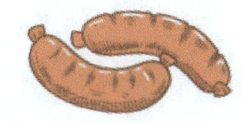

"Rufus... breakfast. We have saved you some sausages, so wake up..."

The little dachshund opened his eyes.

He was home, curled up on the old blue sofa in the kitchen, his iPaw by his side. His humans were sitting around the kitchen table having breakfast.

Rufus stretched and gave himself a big shake. He was seriously hungry.

"Goody, goody, sausages for breakfast. And then I'll find Christopher. I have so much to tell him."

"Oh no, blow it, it's raining."

He could hear the rain on the windows... and felt that old fear in his tummy. The rain was pouring down. That was no good. "So disappointing. No playing with Christopher today."

Then he remembered.

"Hang on a minute – of course I can. I've flown high in the sky, been through snow, swung through rain forests, swum with Jojo and all the cousins." His tummy felt excited. "Yes, yes, yes," he said.

He could hardly wait to get out into the garden and play with Christopher. It was raining. It was wet. Very wet. Who cares. It was going to be so much fun.

Sausages first of course!

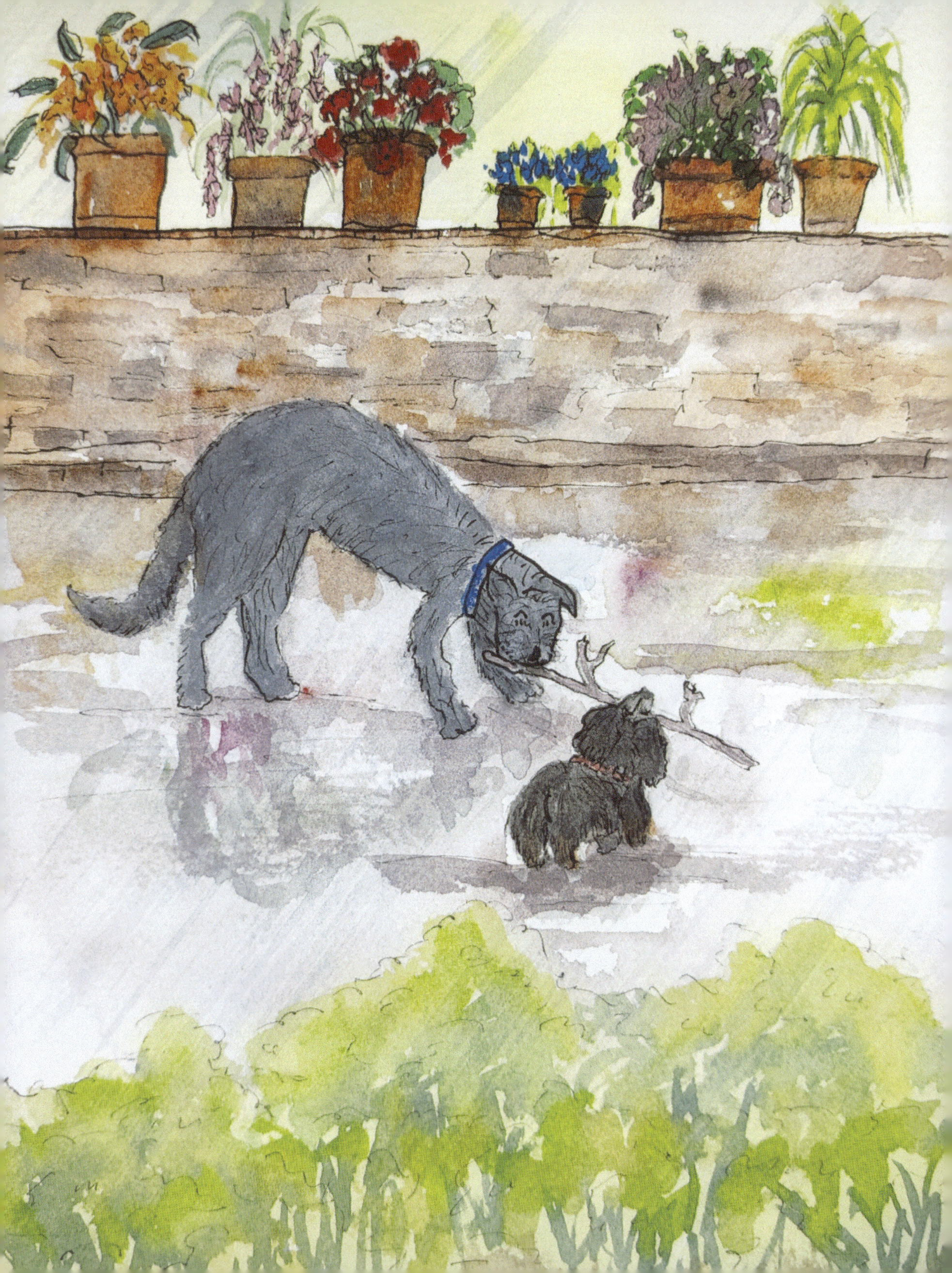

BEING OUT IN THE RAIN

"Being out in the rain is great fun
I can pee and bathe all in one
My paws are so clean
I am the smartest hound you have seen
Being out in the rain is great fun!"

MEET SARAH GREEN

My claim to fame is that I share my birthday on the same day as the late Queen. I love that connection. Born in London, I grew up outside Liverpool and went to boarding school at a very early age, then studied Russian at Nottingham University. I lived in Iran until being evacuated during the revolution and moved to Venezuela.

Coming back to London in 1980, I met my husband and in 1993 we moved to the United States, first to Kansas City which we loved, and ten years later to a small farm in Virginia. It was there that I got the idea of writing about Rufus and his 'rain phobia'. From his early days when taken out to pee he would simply stand there trembling, give me that forlorn look known to any dog owner, and not budge an inch. Gradually he could cope under my umbrella. And slowly he would explore a bit more each time. I admired his stubbornness but mostly that he took his own time to accept the rain. And even to swim. We returned to England in 2019 to be closer to family and friends. And to meet new friends. Although now living with Alzheimer's Disease I love my life and feel very blessed, not least to have Rufus in it.

MEET FRANCES ISAACS

I was born in 1946 and grew up in Hampstead in the house that had belonged to Edward Elgar when he had a London patron. In 1967 I married Barrow and had two sons, Benjamin and Edward and a daughter-in-law, Elena and lastly, our family dog, Moxie. I was a fundraising consultant, working in education largely with a specialist interest in charitable taxation and was involved in bringing the Gift Aid scheme to fruition.

We moved to the Brecon Beacons in the 1990's and in retirement I began to paint. After my diagnosis of Posterior Cortical Atrophy, I despaired until I was shown that there is a good, but different life to be led. I began to teach others with dementia how to relax and lose themselves through painting with watercolours. I worked with Bradford and Stirling Universities to help create courses designed for health professionals and volunteers to gain a better understanding of living with dementia and am a member of the Powys Dementia Leads Steering Group.

Being invited to make images to help bring Sarah's story to life has been a wonderful experience. I feel strongly that the collaboration between two people with shared health issues has a very special strength to it. I associate so strongly with the almost subliminal message of Rufus' tale... Overcoming challenges in life. Sarah and I have to do it all the time!

MEET RUFUS

When I was very tiny, I was totally soaked by a huge rainstorm which made me very frightened. I never wanted to get wet ever again.

I was born on Thanksgiving Day, in 2013, in the foothills of the Blue Ridge Mountains of Virginia.

However, the real thanksgiving day of my life was when Sarah picked me out from my brothers to go and live with her on her farm with lots of fields and woods to run and scamper in - except when it rained of course.

I loved that Sarah was there to take me out to pee under her umbrella, showed me that playing in snow was fun and taught me how to swim. I found that rain and getting wet was not such a big deal after all. This is probably just as well because in 2019 Sarah, David and I moved to England, and nobody told me how much it rained there!

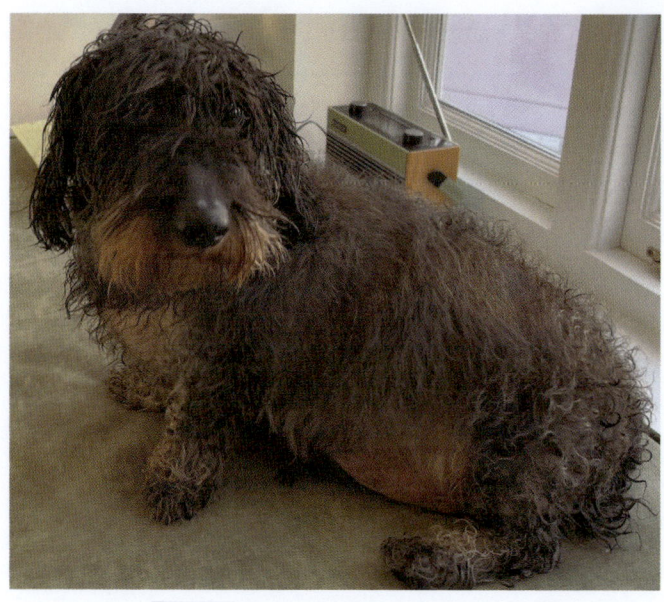

Me after being out in the rain!

Printed in Great Britain
by Amazon